QuantaEssence

Shirley Elias

Independently published by
Shirley Elias
www.quantaessence.com

ISBN 979-8-218-60989-4
Library of Congress Control Number: 2025902413

Cover design by Erin Brown
First Edition

Printed in the United States of America

For my mother, An homage to love.

For Bob, In love with another
and feeling the love within oneself,
hours pass and not a minute passes.

Give away your love
What do you keep it for,
Hidden who will it help?

I want to write a rhyming poem
about the changes that persist
since that auspicious day in June
when I realized I exist
As Being–
Unlimited emptiness

"You are That"
the guru said–and I got it,
just like that.
Struck by realization, stunned
to realize I Am That

Coin Of the Realm

I could say I've never been happier
or at least felt more relieved.
To know the True Self is to know
death shall have no dominion.

Birth into body carries the
I Am vibration.

Unchanging unfathomable
in the presence of the Beloved,
self (to self)
what more is needed.
No thing is Peace itself.

Enjoy the beauty of the world,
that is the legacy.
The heart, the sage says, opens
outward to the world, inward to Infinity.
Two sides of the same coin,
though neither exists but are dreamt.

Love Song

I am the embodiment of the whole universe
connected to the ingoings and outgoings of
all movements
The very flow of breath
river of air
the watershed of Being
breathes in my veins
Being before mother
Subtler than words
The music of a fiddlehead fern
in a forest unfurling
petals open quiver dissolve in flower
kiss the sun
we are the sun

PLEASE–Don't Tell Me What to Do
A Primer for Progeny of Aged Adults in Free Verse

Don't take care of me–even though
you care for me
Aware of maturity, I enjoy these days
this earned leisure lived
in how it pleases

Don't suggest exercise
I've walked lots of steps in eighty years,
sometimes
when I felt like taking a lie-down, I kept walking
had to

Now I get to choose, no blues for me.
Time spent with myself is so precious,
soon I won't be here
to enjoy this long friendship

Marquez said, "The secret to a good old age is an
honorable pact with solitude."
Alone I honor my long and interesting past
while fully in this miraculous present.
Watching persons change knowing
it's a time-limited pastime
makes it even sweeter.
How did I get to be so lucky?

I admire the objects on the walls and floors
of the house I live in now

the colors and shapes and harmonies
the play of light and shadow,
these material enchantments.
Time to honor my depth.

Don't make decisions for me
even if you're scared, deal with it.
Ask what I intend
with my long experience in living
to know what's right for myself.

Don't suffocate me with attention.
Give me the pleasure of watching you
attend to your life,
your choices and their outcomes
Give me space to bless you.

Your care for me and love
for me is gratifying and mutual.
You're some of my favorite persons—
actually, my favorite—this pleases.
I'm discovering the shape and substance
of older age.
The changes are subtle, gradual, and sudden.

Wrinkles appear overnight—Body wobbles.
Sleep, always loved, becomes cherished
Everything deepens.

This dance with the universe has a new rhythm.
I'm not what I thought I was.

The bands have loosened.
Unlimited is my home.

Winter Fractals

The curved iron deck chairs
are curved with mounds of snow that
look like the King and Queen of France
ensconced on thrones
in their winter palace

Snow hemmed branches carry precisely what
each branch can bear,
form a bower over the mounds.
The white sky deepens and darkens
whiteness greys

Lived Life

Winter arrives on hard winds.
The birds are blown across the sky,
swift delivery.
I ponder old wounds:
soft underbelly of confusion

I never figured this one out:
At 16 I stand in front of the Sugar Bowl,
campus hangout of Brooklyn College,
wondering, "Am I an intellectual?"

All I know are my proclivities:
books, libraries, museums—places I fit in.
Paper, pen—not school.

When I first sat on a cushion
at a Buddhist retreat
I knew: Home

So True

Poised on the lip of older age
Teetering on the balls of familiar feet
prehensile toes
skirt the hems
of decades aft and fore

However much I squint,
unable to see into the concept future

Words are given us
inchoate we grasp at language
to express the inexpressible
and yet hope.

Mere words won't do it,
nor fewer.
Leave the page blank.
How will I communicate

If I can't touch you.
I refuse to live in loneliness
I must tell you
that I love

Mother's Day

Fill the world with happiness
let it burgeon out like
an 18th century petticoat
gathering goodness under its skirts

Let me give praise to Oneness
not-twoness
to the light that spreads invisible
across and under all appearances

Unwavering yet full of waves,
particles of color sparkling
under the rainbow
that one eye can see

Let me give praise to music
That which disappears as soon as heard
and yet lingers in the feeling—
the calm of joy

Let me give praise to this called I,
conjured by thought. Invisible,
demanding, private
and oh so believable

Let me give praise
to all that is dreamt,
real and unreal
by which we live today

Rain

I have lived long
I know the names of things
How gazing out at this jungle of leaves
wet and shining from the rain falling
in my ears and wetting the world
sun diamonds dripping incessant
I enjoy this bright cave of beauty

The sapphire between green
dark and light caught in a wink
rain in the distance
the leaves nearby dancing in wood
To love its miracle without category:
this is this or that
Without naming or knowing—
just its raw beauty
the glittering given

Now

There is a relationship here
a gift to be met
that is of this time now
rooted in matrilineal connection.
Now this mother, this daughter, these women
have the chance and challenge
to meet without artifice,
without the impositions of society,
conditioning.
To be not just mother and daughter
but extraordinary women in their majesty.
Equal, steeped in the (other-cheek) love
their echoes from this womb, this time—
calls back all of their ancestors
and says
"Beloved, we are healing,
we are love itself."

when the rosebush is cut back
the promise of the
rose bloom is ensured

There is some integrity that is
not torn apart by circumstance
but that arises from its instinctual bed to roar
when this thread that cannot be broken
is threatened

How can it be threatened if it cannot be broken
It's another breaking that is feared,
the turning away
from the Eternal, the transparent whole
carried in all its emanations
however hidden or unseen.

This is a strength immeasurable in tons.
It is Self or Substance. It is Love's essence. It is
Eternity.
It is what I Am.
This passing form that has been tortured
and squeezed into girdles and wept on scales,
pinched and prodded and
trained into the acceptable and desired
will pass into

Rot or ash or dirt or chemicals whatever its
material is composed of
and with it the dream
of Shirley—born into What Is, lives as What Is,
and dies into What Is—
Nothing is disturbed by this event

And yet Shirley gets to enjoy the
whole parade
To participate in it one day at a time.
How marvelous.

Then there is beauty:
Rainbow colored lights refracted in a glass lamp
glimpsed as a reflection in a glass door
reflecting the tree and sky in a reflection
of the wide window behind me
reflection within reflection within reflection

Someone said, "It's all made of mirrors." Perhaps
it is
also.

It Is as It Is

A very large woodpecker in the dogwood tree
a dead bird on the doorstep of the patio

A crow expanded and fierce
Huge wingspan ate the dead bird

The death of the dream of a separate self
the end of the lie of a separate self
The illusion bursts—a bubble vanishes
a dream fulfills itself

Bhakti

Devotion
Does it matter to what, to whom?
A capacity maybe even an attribute of Love
arises in the heart as a desire to connect
to offer oneself
to what is worthy
without knowing what that is.
A tendency that drinks
at the wellspring of mystery
A silent attitude of persistent endeavor
that can rise in passion or flow hidden
under cover, enabling one to persevere
because that connection is worth everything.
Ultimately it is Essence
the truth of Being, the fountain of Light
where the devotee quenches her thirst
through all the hours and minutes
and years of silent meditation
when she didn't know it as her Self.
Known, it is more beautiful than ever
and as indescribable.

Wherever I go
whatever is known
is the sense of Presence
That which I thought accompanied me
is the other way around
"I" hitchhiked on the spacious sense of presence

The Valise

Body, the holy, is carrying around
the ideas, beliefs that an I cannot
walk on her own.

She's only a thought, a cluster of thoughts
but now there's a hole in the old valise.
It's brown and it's battered, covered
with stickers of all the events
that have made her feel sick.

It's right in the gut
the hidden compartment
that holds all the fears.
This very I is a fragment that hides
the truth that it doesn't exist.

The valise inherited,
passed down through generations.

Just as the essence of the ocean
is not altered by a violent storm
so the essence of our relationship
remains unaltered by upheaval.

Ocean remains water
relationship rests in Love
nothing of value is changed
truth is unperturbed

The dream, the scene, the characters
seem to move forward in understanding
words and emotions rise and fall
some silences, pauses—mirroring flaws
that float in air.

The storm has its own trajectory—
we ride it out.
Perhaps the shoreline shape shifts,
reveals what's hidden,
sighs with the tide.

Nothing is determined
just a storm ridden out.

The leaves fall and fall
and the earth that gives birth
to it receives it all

The love that has brought all this into being
arrives someplace newish that knows itself

Like rounding a bend in the river
the canoe feeling safely home in new territory
Always heading home.

When stuff goes fallow,
the tree dropping its leaves in the fall—
it reconstitutes itself.
It has the chance to draw up the sap
for its own use
when the time for giving arrives
it has the power to deliver
its love to itself.

No limit, no end to Self
and its processes in appearance.

The I is like the little nut, the acorn
that potentiates the Oak.
It must fall to the ground to split open and
clothe itself in the nurturing soil.
So too with a finite mind.
Every stage is beautiful.

Something is heating in this heart
of sorrow awakened by Ukraine blood
Paternal grandparents and uncles
reaching out.
No one but me remains to remember
on this beautiful spring day.
Grandparents, Aunts, Uncles, Cousins
murdered naked at the edge of a ravine
tumbling into Jewish dust. Indistinguishable
from the dust of others–34,000 etc.
It would have been me, except for birth date

A bright sun dips
behind the tallest tree
pen and book fall in shadow

It's all a play
a dance of the infinite
in endless amusement

Extraordinary autumn day
aging poplar leaves are
waving goodbye

Mothers are amazing
they are the carriers of home
home itself.
Mother's body, ahh to lean against
that square soft shape
yielding but strong.
Hands—hands that shape and pat
knead and oily press my face—cheeks

Hold—mother carries the centuries
ancestral cells sing the notes
between us—ancient melody

Divine Mother—I almost forgot thee
in my search for consciousness
But I can never take the teachings
of a man and be complete—whole

Divine Mother it is you I am in Love
with my Self us we are One

Why not, why not enjoy it this a.m. at 9:15
I could be in a car right now
hustling along to West Asheville to park,
switch cars—at least switch the carcass
and be transported to Black Mountain
to sit in a circle in satsang,
gaze and wait for teacher's arrival and
experiences that enlighten and convince,
"There is no you."
It's a lot of trouble to go through to be erased
at least persuaded of my erasure.

It's a funny thing to do
a form to convey formless
a group to dissolve separateness
huddled together at the top of a treacherous
road to say "No one's here, nothing's happening."
Why bother?
something to do, some belonging ritual.
I have, it seems, nothing to share
no one here.
I am completely unimportant, irrelevant,
a leaf in the wind.

But to myself—ah—that's another story.
Enchanted by experience I participate gratefully
in this unfoldment
without really caring about any of it

Movement natural to the form
stillness behind the raindrops
Shakti dances

The Fragrance of My Soul

The first time I knew there was a perfume
that arose from the body was the scent
of strawberries on the lips of K after he
had made oral love to me. "That was
from you," he said when I asked about
the fragrance. I thought "Venus lives
in me."

"Silence is golden,"
all we need to be safe.

What is safety? An idea.
A concept of Paradise
forever lost to Eve
a bluff.

If I had remained
swaddled in ignorance
I would still be afraid

Song Psalm

When all our bitterness is swept away
and we are left with only love
upon our lips and toes
then we will know why we came here:
To breathe pure light and dance in air.
Like a giant broom this hand of God
will make all dark things clear

"The shell–like covering which our souls have excreted to house themselves, to make for themselves a shape distinct from others, is broken, and there is left of all these wrinkles and roughnesses a central oyster of perceptiveness, an enormous eye."

-Virginia Wolfe, *Street Haunting*

What's seen is what's seeing

Dogwood's berries are nascent white
peeking out between mature leaves
tipping vermillion, wet with rain.
Soon robins will be swarming the tree
feasting on the bright red berries.
Last year, a single berry remained
and then that too was gone.

I envy those who died
peacefully, preferably
no more to do—work completed

Awareness would have me be alive
still—there is gratitude
and willingness along with envy

Sigh… it just goes on and on
moving objects from one house to another.
When will it ever end

I'm so tired of these objects

In time all things pass
how clever that is
how ineffable is source

A lone bird, so small
on a swaying branch
all the company I need

All The News That Fits The Page

It's meaningless
if not for the suffering
we could be laughing our heads off

An art installation in Rotterdam
Four sculptures of fecal matter
sat on elegant Persian rugs

The human birthday cake
Artists arranged in a circle
with candles coming out of their assholes

Elaborate toothwork exhibition in London
Mayans drilled holes in their teeth and set in
precious stones
Fifty thousand corpses, after the battle of
Waterloo

St. Apollonia jumped in the fire rather than
renounce her faith
Though they shattered her teeth in 24 hours

I live in This
imaginary and real
the mystery itself

The Meaning of Being

I clothe myself in body
I cloak myself in mind
then doing does itself
because I am in time
and peace occurs in emptiness
the faces that are love
and space whirls round the galaxies
and I am lost and found

an empty road
the tablecloth of sky
unfurled its revelation

I feel joy—maybe yoga—maybe book
Maybe not working
Maybe alive.

I say a prayer silently—offering
myself to universal consciousness to
do with me as it will in a sort of
surrender—and realize the surrender
is a kind of bowing to the light.
To love, to God—to whatever is
highest and best—to what I am
and beyond. And in the same moment
hope to realize that. It is an attitude
of perpetual surrender,
bowing in gratitude and Love,
radiating through all my actions
and words throughout the day and night.
It is like the sun, always shining.
Its very nature is Light
My very nature is Love and gratitude.
Filled with the Light.
Living in the Light.
The Light of consciousness,
the Light of God's Love.

Being. That is all there is ♡

deep sea waters flow
many ways at once
oceanic harmony

I keep seeing his waxen body with
its perfectly pedicured toes.
Not like the fungus crusty toes of life
and he is Well Dead—no breath escapes
his open mouth.
Though bristles on his cheeks—unshaven
I remember
urging him to shave because his smooth face
looked so much younger

He couldn't care less now—nor I.

I tried to summon some deep feeling—
grief—by touching and looking
All I came up with was panic when
his wallet and keys seemed missing.

When I left the room I said goodbye
to no one

Later, in the apartment, all was ease.
He was clearly present, unperturbed
glad to see us
His daughter and me estranged through life
bonded through his death.
I was glad too for this miracle

Fifty-two days later I don't know what I feel
These two deaths, tethers in life,

have left me free.
My hair is greying and growing—
no artificial applications

I live more in the light—fulfilling my purpose
Sick for sixteen days, I hibernated—
exalting in silence

Still, I wait.
Awareness moves the me. Already dead.

I have lived the last 58 years of this
life as a mother and I didn't even
know that this condition—motherhood,
was defined, shaped and imposed by
environment, culture, society, history,
belief, fear, need, expectation,
desire, loss, pride, shame, guilt,
myth, story, religion, and has
been the defining underlying cage of life
lived as Shirley.

This whole motherhood fantasy
is falling to pieces—
sharp edges of the puzzle tear
my intestines—the imaginary womb.
I nurtured and nourished my children
with the dictates of nature—
where the swelling belly of their home
was inside me—
as long as I was safe they were safe.

There was no Shirley to contend with
as long as I stopped smoking and drinking
that womb was unaffected by me.

I was part of a long history of mother
matrix for which this body was
perfectly suited.
And the first years of birth, of milk—
and childhood and diapers and crying—

and laughing and kisses and hugs—
the bliss of union—mine to remember.
Many jump-puddles along the way
errors and mistakes along with
care and devotion and love
and overwhelm.

Where does motherhood end
This fantasy of perfect love
this shield of protection, guidance—
this made up expectation—
this myth.
When can I just be me—as I am
and know that is enough in every relationship
Especially my relationship with Love,
and if I cause disappointment, so be it.
I will not judge myself if I am honest
and true and know the clear ring of kindness.

I'm not putting someone else ahead of me
or me ahead of someone else—
just responding as the situation arises
however flawed the response.
As awareness I am unlimited
as body-mind, sadly and gladly so.

All this will be forgotten in time—
swept into the great vastness
the intention of the universe deems
These molecules having done their work

will merge into the sweep
May I remember this as story unfolds

"Out of a whole lifetime, by God, sometimes the only thing that saves a person is error, and I know that we shall not be saved so long as our error is not precious to us."

    -Clarice Lispector

I don't know what I'm feeling—
that is, a great deal of feeling is
happening
Love and grief and sadness and acceptance
in the air, in the atmosphere
in the hemisphere
This is the return of light
the rainbow streams this morning
on the yoga mat
the wrapping up the years
the Love of the Light

Consciousness, my Self—provides the energy
the story, the play, in Shirley and
the birds, the body, the daughter,
the money, the years, the friends,
life the great force—goes on.
Gratitude for Mia arises every moment.
What karma is she fulfilling,
what life continues to live itself out
as us, now?

This bond is eternal
is all one
Outshoots of rainbow light stream
through our eyes as the sun
the star shines

My Life Is a Quiet Ocean

From the depths the waves
surface, flutter in wind
whitecaps froth, surf, tease the shore

Feelings like music arise and
land on particles of light
Rise and descend
Rise and descend

I watch from someplace fathoms below
the movement
still
silent
dark

On Reading Merwin's *The Last Garden*

All of us poets
it is not the first time
although we wish it to be last

Had I known earlier I would not
have taken the Bodhisattva vow
"To return again and again 'til all
beings are enlightened."

Now I don't give a fig for enlightenment

A good massage precluding a peaceful
sleep, and a dream of a newborn

Do not weep for me when I am gone
unless you must to give your heart ease.
I learned to be continuous
on this go 'round.
What is buried is transparent.
Through breast nurtured and womb planted
like the tree whose seed fell to earth
and grew to majestic size.
So we made thee and thou and
you grew too.
The clouds that pass with laughing faces
and too skinny legs disintegrate,
reform, disappear
Do you mourn them?

The voice that writes these words
has no author
they go with me when I am gone
Feast on these crumbs for just a minute
then turn your attention to
the sumptuous repast
that has your name. There be nourished.

woven story capacity
some are meant to know this
all are This

All these are thoughts
Behind it, emptiness

The ones I used to tell
are gone—along with me.
Now knowing is enough.

The one who used to wave her arms
calling "look at me"
is memory.

I visited
my dying friend in solace.
"May I hold your hand?" I asked
He gave it.

We sat and focused
on the flowing energy.
I read Rumi aloud

What is the purpose, the meaning
I used to ask, waiting
for the answer

Now I am eighty-one
in love with my grey hair
wild again but this time
only myself

You suffer heartbreak and then
it all gathers into human experience
Remembered–the ember sparked
by a story, a song

You remember your own experience,
leaving children, husband, home
and then–
you wouldn't trade this moment now
for anything remembered
not regretted, just a little rue

Everything you ever had is still yours,
had only in thought
Eventually everything goes but not
now while you're breathing above ground

So far along and you hardly traveled
anywhere

Cast off these shrouds
that you are not
open to the emptiness you are

Freedom From Self

A mind free of self
crystal prism
light of awareness
dances in form

When the pen is moving I disappear
I the conscious awareness
of being

always going deeper to become
completely clear
transparent
Transparency

nothing in the way
whole
seamless
knowing

Awareness

These 3 a.m. awakenings,
the uncontrolled images
unspool upon the open no-place
of awareness

Now, not next
not then either
Right now what is
pure awareness present

Prepositions describe relationship
in-of-to
with nothing separate
Does that make sense?

In meditation
Instruction arises
from silence
"Lose the words."

We are free
we are not alone
we were never separate
desperation is a choice

Flower of higher complexity
consciousness on two feet
awareness breathing, beloved.
Life living Itself

Not a collection of moribund souls
faithfully following worn paths
into the killing fields
whether by cannon or can't

Evolution is in the air

How did I dare get married
Fell into it like the hole in the
life saver

Somehow it worked out.
The wound repairs itself given time
the progress marked—day by day:
discoloration, puckering, shiny taut.

Eventually a small white scar
to note location.
No-one's doing

I'm so in Love
Love fills the space like Light
Love carried by Light, One.

Will the dogwood fully bloom?
Interest, curiosity, caring.
The answer already written
though not yet discernible

I am a being of time,
That's what happened.

Unexpected Warm Spring Day

The scent of my skin
in the sunburnt air (transforming)

Dark red flowers dangling from thin branches
The great maple framed against
a Carolina blue sky.
Awakening to spring.

Not too distant, the mountain—
sister appalachian

In a warm breeze
branches dance shadows on the
patio bricks, sunroom walls.

Wind percussion carries the
fleeting chorus of hidden birds
The soft scratches of the pen harmonize
the heartbeat, breath
the neighbor's red roof

Brown bird on a fence post
vibrating throat song pierces the air

utterly itself.
The breeze caresses neck, shoulders
ruffles the hair.

Hello, hello—
A turkey vulture circles the sky.
Somewhere, a siren.

The great pleasures of life:
Picking up a library book on hold
shopping the supermarket, eggs on sale–
everyone masked.
Backing into a car in the lot–making a dirty noise
The driver, a ruddy man pulls out
the fender and says, "It's okay."

Dvorak's 7th on the radio
a cup of tea
a pen, a notebook, and mild rain

I went for a Covid test today after exposure
a fucking rigamarole to negotiate
I feel fine, though a little off balance
'what if...' and 'this is the end.'
I'll finish my book first

Forget everything you ever thought
you knew and open to reality.
Tap into your power to see the
invisible—seeing through,
not with, your eyes.
Hearing through,
not with, your ears.
Gut knowing—that great
empty space between the ribs
in which the heart floats
in a sea of air
A mighty vessel of God's
armada.

Awareness animates. Creates. Makes.
Known Itself as all there is—and we
body, mind and world—
Its playthings.
Even as I sit here in this peaceful funny
world, I am a thought. All is well.
I serve that I Am.

Covid

Here's to the weirdest Christmas ever.
Where no one gathers and no gifts exchanged,
where each of us at home without a stocking
send Christmas cheer from heart to heart alone.

I'm reading Paul Celan's "Death Fugue"
Translated from German
When I get a text message from my daughter
"Good morning my wonderful Momma!"
"I woke up really clear and
feeling great today!
Can't wait to tell U about it!
May try you at noon when I get a break
It's AMAZING out!
Enjoy this gift of a day!"

Celan was born Paul Antschel in 1920
to German-speaking Jewish parents in
Czernowitz.
My parents met in Czernowitz, fell in love.
Married in Czernowitz,
begot sister Marcia in Czernowitz in 1928.
So you can say I'm begotten in Czernowitz.

On July 6, 1942 German & Romanian
nazi troops invaded Czernowitz.
Burned the city's great synagogue
murdered nearly seven hundred Jews
within three days
Three thousand by the end of August.

Ten years after my parents emigrated
(at my father's insistence and good fortune)
I was born in Williamsburg, Brooklyn—
innocent of death camps.

Paul Celan was fifty when he
suicided in 1970
(I was 32, just began Psychoanalysis—
 a new life.)
Who can say.
It's all arranged—and so random.

There's no one holding the world together.
The universe is one body
our body is the universe—Her body

What does it feel like to be a cell,
a drop of ocean, a point of light
Like your self, that's what.
Non-existent alone
and yet the thought—me, prevails.

Today the snow—fierce winds that shake
the evergreens
make a swishy sound, ladies in ball gowns.
Keeping the heat at 72°— perfect temperature
year-round in San Diego.
Where am I exactly? I mean
exactly— longitude & latitude
on the map of the world.

Besotted.
That's how I like to be.
Besotted with the beauty
of the natural world.

Remembering the tiny orange shells
along the shore in Morton's Cove.
Falling down in awe
and gratitude.

Gypsy girl's moon arrived.
Bob inhaled my radiance
his mouth rimmed with grape juice
Bedazzled.

I've been trying to articulate the value of the
silent power of pregnancy, birth and nursing.
No man can understand this—
no awakening deny it.
Cloud to mountain, mingling.

In an act of generosity, a woman allows
penetration.
Carries a being within her body-being,
releases this self of herself
flesh of her flesh, feeds with her own fluids
nurtures and lets go.

This is what God does. Lends Her being to
human development
lives through it, loves it, plays through it
nurtures with abundance and all manner of life,
then lets go.

Nothing belongs to it.
Neither possession or clinging.
It is generosity and detachment.
It is Love giving itself to itself.
Augmenting Itself.
Imperishable.

Essence as alive awareness.
Essence is alive awareness.
Unlimited borderless presence being.
Life living Itself.

Imagine if everybody saw at once
saw the Truth
What an explosion of Light!
(all 7 billion of us)

It has nothing to do with me
and yet the pleasure is mine

I'm nothing, nowhere,
life lived so far comes to this:
only appearance

my mother appears
when I look in the mirror:
Love notes her absence

When writing I feel great pleasure
in being myself. This being
cannot conform with spiritual
correctness but must be true to Itself.
This was always the case
but before I knew
I belonged to the world and the source
there was complication.
Now I cannot listen to correctness or
even expression that claims
Ultimate truth.
I have to trust myself
the intuition and consciousness
the direct pipeline to what is, to reality.
This is not my mind, which is a
conditioned patterning—but truth
that reveals itself to the open
Presence. Self-truth.

Note to Children

"Sink into the heart of awareness"
Ramana said. This understanding
appears gradually,
unfoldedness is a condition—
a fluid condition of being.
Gradual openness into the unlimited truth.
Life finding Itself home already
again and again.
Oh my beloved children—you
enrich my life by opening my heart
to the immense love your being
generates. All of love and
happiness is in your presence
here on earth with me. I
thank you again and again for
choosing this vehicle now. I
love you more than words can say
and feel your love in reciprocity.
Continual blessings.

Surely I know nothing, have
no answers, care not for questions
anymore. Slowly, silently
Knowing reveals itself to itself
and since I am That, it works.
Something hears.

Hop on the R&R Uncertainty
take any available seat
for the ride of your life.
No destination
you're not even moving.
Enjoy the scenery

What a party!
Wholeness in every particle
All the coats thrown on the bed
Most take their own home

I feel like the spider woman
Sitting here sending out tendrils
of hope and good vibrations to
loved ones in turmoil,
long strands of light reaching to
New Jersey and Rhode Island.
Smaller local webs only minutes
not hours away.

From my fingertips shimmering rays
are extending into the atmosphere.
Thought vibrations barely language
go out to Israel along the
double helix spiral.
Strangers appear at the door
bearing the same name as the one
I believed was on the way
and is the perfect visitor
to fill the bill.

Nothing I need to do but align,
attune to the Truth
and realize I Am That

All the rivers of the world are
connected through the flow of
their vibrations to the endless sea.
Frequencies beyond human hearing
create a melody that says:
Mother Earth, Mother Earth

So too with the bloodstreams of
the body. Carrying the song
of self through the toes and fingertips
to all the bloodstreams of the
human race and beyond.
Singing the song "I Am, I Am"

And it is one giant song–
a symphony of myriad creatures
with no orchestration but itself
that ebbs and flows in concert
with the rays of sun and
phases of the moon.

Tune in–tune in to the song
of yourself–in convergent harmony
with all you are, all that is
in endless flow

Love is the strongest power in the
universe—all energy and movement
flows from love and as love
and needs no motive
but itself.

An astounding discovery was
that love augments itself.
Thus when I was willing to
love again—and tested it
by a kiss in the kitchen where I had
loved and grieved my dead
true love—I found to my
astonishment that I loved him
still more by loving another. That
love is not limited
nor time bound

The Holocaust

When I could locate the human heart
within the soul it became possible to transmute
the horror and pity into compassion.
No longer personal but a deep relatedness
with my ancestry, DNA inheritance,
the love and peace that I Am.
The body-mind, the Story of Shirley,
remembered the trauma
but no longer took it personally—
while it continues to inform and encompass
the universal,
I love
for the beauty of sensitivity—
and your smile.

So discovering that I am not
what I thought I was
a person, whole, complete to herself,
I disperse–thin out and spread
like atmosphere over waves
of being alive
just so.

Small bird landed atop the highest
needle of a branch on the
highest tree
aimed right for it—it seemed.
Landed, rested a while
gazed about— (I thought)
then plummeted fearlessly down
into thin air—
and disappeared from view.
Could you do that?

How Am I Absolved of Responsibility?

I did not come here to do something,
be something in the eyes of society,
not be somebody. That I came with
no mission. Born of spontaneity and
randomness within the DNA matrix
I am just an expression of life, lived
and living here now.
What develops, what arises out of
the play of consciousness as this form
is not Shirley's business.
This called Shirley, body-mind,
grew in a matrix of social conditions—
widening from family, to friends,
to neighborhood, culture, world.
And a concept, a picture or structure
formed in the brain-body-mind,
Shirley called I existing as a
hard nugget inside the awareness
I Am.

Then came—I am what? Later,
much later came I Am That—since then
that has come to be understood
as this—what is—without the
hard nugget of the idea or belief
in a Shirley like this—the narrative
of experience—the story of

Shirley—while interesting is not
what was, is, and remains after

the form and story are inferred.
I'm not that important is the first freedom.
I'm not needed or necessary is understood
and I will be placed where it's divined.
That is relied upon and trusted.

So it's not that there's not a
me—it's that the me is irrelevant
to life functioning and going on
as it does.
Sometimes it seems the I has a
say but it's usually after the fact—
The brain is a few millimeters
behind the occurrence.

Basically what I am is a witness
to experience and experience itself.
The play, and the audience and the players,
as Shakespeare wrote.

I'm falling slowly like leaves
gently hitting the ground
reality.
The bright colors of Autumn
fade into a carpet of earth tones
soft underfoot.
I don't give a damn

We love the absolute, the Ultimate—
The deep black void that upholds
the universe, the nothing
out of which I am something.
Creature of time and all its glories
and brutality, the impersonal one
or, not-two.

And there is Love for this humanness,
this sweet sensitivity that walks around
and can fall into the hole of ignorance
to be rudely awakened once more,
and again—and can laugh.
This laughter is human, and these tears—
all part of the game.

This morning the dream was a funeral.
A box too short for a daddy—but
it was he—and before that sisters
who excluded me. Where are they all now?
Gone, like puffs of smoke and
soon, me too, this writer here—a
memory for a while soaring up and out
and over as light vibrations among
This whole imagined scene.

I am life happening
consciously living itself
observable by nature, the trees
bared of leaves
fallen to ground.
The visible blue space of sky
the eye viewing the hand holding
the pen, writing.
The child, now grown to womanhood
sobbing briefly in my arms and
going forth to conquer another day.
The mother, home in her sweats
deepening.

Today, friends on zoom, writers
pouring their hearts into words,
sharing. This is what humans do
women—no longer baboons
also life happening, albeit with
bananas on branches
swinging.

Erasure, a swath of paint across a canvas
and I'm gone
but let me go out
enjoying.

The sun is warm
the wind roars
last Sunday of November.
Runaway leaves scattered across
the damp ground
I sit here season into season
tracking the sun's trajectory across the sky
All directions open to view
this cherished spot of earth.

Graceful and bowing the pine boughs revering
the wind that strengthens the trunks.
All works together, the harmony of
One taste

This is the only day
Here I breathe.
Here I talk to my son.
Here I attend to tax anxiety,
"Did I mess up,
   will it be costly?"

My accountant is dead.
Here I am soothed, drink tea, eat veggies,
write, walk on the greenway.
Here I walk without the cane
Here I carry the cane for safety
Here I am 84 years young
Hee–Haw

Try to convince someone that their
experience–mostly thought–is false
A closed mind, or a mind holding
on to itself for dear life is unapproachable.
Stubbornness becomes obstinacy,
an ass.

Don't argue or agree. Remain neutral
"It seems that's your experience."
When all the benchmarks have slipped away
it must be terrifying.

When people get the idea that things are
"spinning out of control" it's just that
things, substratum and world, are as
usual but that the mechanism that
believes itself to be I is
losing the ability to hold on
to its version of reality.

Everything's spinning already—
it's gravity that provides the illusion that
we're standing still. The stillness
that underlies appearance is what
is not spinning. Spinning is a manifestation—
not something to be held on to.

How long will it take for that woodpecker
to take down the maple tree?
How many generations of woodpeckers?

Brooklyn Flower

Banks of Forsythia, crest on the wave
of Earth's belly, stands her ground
impervious to the gardener's shears.
Within wild naked branches
Seeds of light lay dreaming
through winter's long indrawn breath.
Forsythia is not waiting;
flowering is not her aim.
But at a secret signal,
nascent burning sealed within her Being
Bursts into fragrant yellow flowers;
An offering and a triumph.
Let go, it's all arranged through hidden depth
and power,
The One eternal Love you are mirrors
Forsythia's flower.

Trust In Unfolding

Rainbows End sparkles, erupts
in points of brilliant color
unfathomable from the tiny bud
squeezed petal on petal.

Where is the scent?
In the rose?
In the nose?
Neither are correct.

Like the anemone,
the rose, its heart exposed
before the petals fall.

Outstretched full width arms
breadth exceeds the banyan tree:
In this way I touch the sky,
the ocean bottom
and the root of the rose bush.

This wanting thing is I
yet no such I is
anywhere to be seen

I thoughts constantly reinforce
themselves, building
a silt barricade

Yet there's something wordless
saying what it is
revealing itself

The Twins

Out of love come these two
glowing little noses in the womb.
Rosa and Levi developing side by side
forming limbs and organs they will need
to live in a world of their making.

How they are silent, mouthing sounds
only Tessa can hear as they turn
inside her body, hidden from eyes.
Soon, soon they will appear to us,
ready for the adventure of life on earth.

We delight in them, their bodies,
and their equipment to clutter up the house.
Heaven on earth,
the birth of these loved beings!
I wait to enfold them in love,
the very love that brought them out of emptiness.

When this heart opened, releasing
the precious jewel of essence
the radiance spread and
dissolved into the everything
it had longed for and I
began to disappear into the
Already.

To be Love's servant and
Love itself—to know love
by being love, that is
enough.

I dreamed I needed a new car
and chose a Dodge Dart
Small, insignificant, cheap
and I'm a millionaire

Let me proclaim my glory

See how the fallen leaves stick to the tall cedar
like Christmas decorations
A golden sun radiates shimmering rainbows
and lemon limned forsythia leans forward to be
embraced.
The so-called "invasive" tiny pear tree ripens
to feed multitudes of robins
Mama maple has turned her green leaves
yellow tinged red
while russet mountains line the sky
blue above
How gracious the seeing.

The leaves fall and fall
and the earth that gives birth to it
receives it all.

Now I am unwinding.
Like the wind shaking the remaining leaves of
the mama maple, the fragments and events of this
long life are loosening and falling
to the ground, 'til nothing remains.

Such a rich tapestry of events and extensions.
All that seemed to be me flying through
marriages, divorce, separation,
falling in love, falling out of love,
working, school—so much school; confusion, loss,
gain, belief, sorrow, joy, wanting, getting, taking,

comparing, OMG what a waste, use, expenditure
of time. Travel, foreign countries, California,
NYC–my home–now the mountains
and it's all finished.

Just now I see that this was some human drama
enacted, scripted, determined without ever really
knowing I was fortune's plaything. That's Dame
Fortune, a name for the unidentifiable substance,
consciousness that runs the show.

No meaning beyond the human heart and
curiosity–and not a moment of regret because
there is no separate me that could have done
anything different than what occurred, or occurs.
Thought would have it that there's an I who
chooses and it's still weird because I'm certainly
here but awareness of what happens lags a second
or milliseconds behind what happens. The
experience, thought, feeling or perception is
known after it takes place so I can believe I
choose because I think so, but
I'm not the separate self
I believed myself to be.

I'm something else that's not individual,
autonomous, personal, separate.
I'm more like the awareness of the wind

that shakes the branches and witnesses
the falling leaves.

And If It Is True...

That there is a soulmate
then there is a soul
and it's not in a person
but in a cloud of unknowing
that has been caught in the current
moving through the ocean of being eternally,
so be it

And if it is true
that there are cycles and ends to cycles
and then beginnings of new cycles
and we have come together now
to finish and move on
or somehow help each other and ourselves
to ascend,
so be it

And if it is true
that I, whoever I may be
need to relate in ways that are not the old ways—
that under the umbrella of Awareness
there are no old ways anymore existing—
then not I, but allowing what wants to move,
desire that is impersonal
to come to its own conclusion,
so be it

And if it is true
Lord, keep me out of the way, I pray
with my wants and imagined needs
my sticky addictive mind and greedy habits
keep me in gratitude and faith
remembering, "It's all arranged,"
to live fulfilled in longed for peace,
so be it

I worried about the dogwood tree
In autumn there seemed to be few
red berries
In spring
branches empty of blossoms.
When the tips of leaf buds began
some delicate sprigs appeared naked

Now green leaves of the dogwood tree flourish,
are abundant and harmonize with the wind

How foolish the I that worried
and how tender

I love being in, looking out
Sheltered and exposed

O Beloved–do I serve you well enough?
I know this game is temporary
but it is all there is now.
Knowing the truth–or Truth–I Am
nothing is in the way of the way
But I am so well used to doing it seems
the thinking pattern wants something done.
Knowing is enough
but I don't mind doing if it's natural
effortless effort, as long as I am
following your will which is simply
the slipstream of living.
There is no me to exalt.
I meet the slings and arrows
with curious disinterest.
Nothing personal–but so much waste
or is that the separate I speaking?
Any opinion is worthless.

Hypatia came across consciousness (yesterday).
Neoplatonism–this need of men to
categorize and name ideas and constructs
But I resonated to her name and
will investigate further.
Spinoza was mentioned–and there is resonance.

So many are ignorant with little or
no light leaking through the chinks
in their armor.

To Live in The Light

In October 1981 I died in hypnotic regression.
As an old woman I awoke with eyes still closed
to the brightness of a thousand suns, endless and
deep.

The Light completely filled all with Itself.
It was total.
In deep silence the question of my purpose
was communicated and answered,
"To live in the Light."

I filled with great joy then
thinking and feeling I knew my purpose,
though I actually had no understanding
of what that meant. But it was
a starting point, however veiled in ignorance.

It was never I, and the way forward
never me but the lights were
blinking on and those who would be
guiding the way were lining up.

I hear a clap of thunder
and joy arises.
The leaves sing in the wind
and I'm in love.
Today a squirrel and I met eye to eye,
high branch to ground.

I told Mel "When I'm 85 I'll eat
whatever I want."
I lived a life of foolishness
as if there was a me relating to
a body which was mine.
Convoluted mentality

Yet somehow something guides this Isness,
hears its foolish pronouncements
and continues anyway.
This immensity
is utterly reliable.

We make things,
humans are makers.

To be living in the Light
is to be connected
or more than connected,
to be based in Love.
The essence of being alive
is as a vibration, a wave,
a body-mind form, an expression,
an emanation of Source
endowed with and by consciousness
to live out this appearance
that both is and isn't the self.
Like light I am boundless,
non-material and cannot be grasped.

It's so nice to settle in one place
and to throw out the garbage twice a week

Things go wrong—flooding, discomfort,
disorder—nothing tragic—movement

Awareness moves not—
the turning of the Earth. It all turns
together and at once
Nothing separate from the whole enchilada
Cosmos for dinner

I'm part of it, eternally.

Ravages of Aging

Aloneness heads the list
in the parade of passing days.
The line stretches back beyond the eye
eighty-four years of days.

Stretches back like a line of ants
sometimes carrying a boulder,
sometimes a log across a stream
but marching on, one by one, in
an unbroken line of passage.

Only today is lived—
here is where the aloneness calls itself.
Here is the silence and the rooms
here are the objects and the subjects
here is the openness in which
thought intrudes.
Here is the hand holding the moving pen
here is the alpha and the omega
Always here
until there is no more.

Sitting here like a toad
upon her throne
I cast seeds of well-being into the atmosphere
Catch that one and let it grow
in your heart mind.
Watered with laughter
we all share the joke

Oh, magic mushroom—
lens to underlying truth and beauty
Inspiration

True Love

I'm having that "in love" feeling
Excited, full.
Celebration going on inside
my head
Dancing, singing, silently.

A faint scent of burnt
and the leaves dangling,
shaken by the light wind
a breeze, really
Zephyr.

Is that boy calling me from
the beyond that is so close
He wouldn't forget me–us.
There's no forgetting us.

Without past, future, time or space
Where is there to go?

This person I thought I was
or had to be, now gone
while I'm still alive.

Consciousness makes you think
you're something with
"I am this," and "I am that"
And you go on believing 'til someone
(who thinks he's something too)
lays this body in the ground or
burns you up

This is the biggest magic trick of all
in the magic show of trees,
and plants, and animals, and us!

But the heart is real. Or seems so—
certainly feels a lot
and reaches back into the void
beneath, above, around us all
and keeps hoping.

Maybe AI is a good idea—
an idea whose time has come.
Moved by the heart, by love.
It cannot be worse than what we've wrought.
And everything good, we didn't make that
anyway.

Full Moon in Aries

Shirley dear,
do not lose faith. Life will continue
to be as interesting and challenging as ever—
albeit surrounded by an aura of peace and
happiness due to your enfoldment in
conscious awareness. Life as you know it
will continue to unfold unexpected.
Meetings and revelations will hold you
in their arms just as the trees do. Keep
open heart and soul and know that
every day, every moment, is arranged for
your benefit and well-being. Live in the
Light and continue to love and trust your
inner knowing—it is what you are and
will keep you safe and happy and your
children—all your children—safe and happy.
Thank you. I love you fully, totally with
all my being, every shred of it.
Thank you.

Autumn is here, winter is coming!
Exciting to know this happening.
Better even to write words, with a pen!
Who is writing
and simultaneously reading
These occurrences are amazing!
How did this happen

Not to know. Call it this and that:
consciousness, awareness, presence.
Words hint at the goings-on,
but no explanation.

Little cells and molecules jumping
around in this so—called body.
Brain firing off synapses (so—called).
Plenty of activity—call it mind.

But this delight at being,
eating breakfast and noticing the changes
in light and temperature
the experience of other autumns and winters
the familiar cycle 85 times is a thrill!

Just this:
awareness
How wonderful!

Love augments Itself.
The first great discovery!
It has nothing to do with I or me
deciding who and how much to love
and what I can allow myself
in good conscience.

It has nothing to do with me ever.
Love is her own master.
She seeks only to express her infinitude.
Flowing like an endless river,
she gives and gives and gives.
In all seasons and at all times
she knows no boundaries,
no conventions
Seeks only to be known.

I am her vessel.
You too are this, if you allow it—
disappearing into her arms
and whatever you held dear before,
give it up. Surrender.
You will not be sorry if you
choose to be chosen.

Fulfillment is inherent in how we're made.

> "In out the petal knows
>   the curved lines of the petalled
>   rose."
>   -*Virginia Bagliori*

Traveling On the Edge of The Ocean

sand shore warm cool day
pebbles shells crunching underfoot
wet warm waves on ankles
Vast open present

When I was a person
I took everything
personally

Totally intimate with the earth.
Young and old at the same time.

The vulnerability that comes with age
Body, eyes, not dependable
as they once were.
Fogginess over the whole experience
of driving in the dark.
Cautionary adjustments–
(parking close by, squinting
 almost blinded by Halogen headlights)
"Maybe I better take an uber."

And yet–so young.
Mind light as air.

The sun is gorgeous hot through the
leafless trees. Only when it
passes the trunk is it obscured
for moments, then it blazes hot
again on my chest and face.
I wish my mother could be sitting
out here in the sun's gaze.
I would bring her a cup of tea.
My beloved mama.

Silence Is All I Endure

The silence, the sun, the shadows
The changing world captures the
senses; the layers of colors
of sky—blue white grey
Paler than color
Waving branches greet the eye
Continual interest
remembering mountains all around.
This natural world is surely a paradise.
We are given so much entertainment.
And it is necessary

The Earth never stands still—
moves continually against the unmoving—
Thinly veiled by the senses.

I AM. Probing the meaning
and depths of the mantra.
Am is Being and I is Knowing—
knowing Being—the gift of birth.

I am essence of a seamless whole
never anywhere.
Though I seem to be here now
and I like it.
It seems to be okay—
no expectations.

The molecule I am—drifting
endlessly in the light of God,
is God. This way.
Being and knowing being.

This amazing awareness
translates happening into experience
and I'm awake in the show.
I am the show.

Be as you are.
There's nowhere to go and nothing to do.

Be what you want.

If you want peace, be peace.
Same for love, kindness, generosity,
happiness, etc.

Longings of the Heart

I feel it, an energy in the
heart chakra.
Mentally I open it
resist the closing,
but allow the closing.
The opening and the closing is the dilation
of the heart pumping blood
and nutrients to the brain.
This is a gift; like the swaying
of branches in the breeze
"The wind inside the wind."
No need to shield this diadem.

In winter the animal body warms itself
with wool and fleece and cocoa.
It's cocoon time; curled into an
apostrophe. Breathing into itself,
warmed by the flowing river.

Trees and birds are brave in winter.
With each snowflake we get to appreciate infinity.
Curled into the earth we remember
the womb
and death.
The endless cycle of Being

Draw back the curtain
of the cosmos
original emptiness stands revealed

The Dream of I

Revenant I pass through days
days pass through I
One whole, alive in emptiness
enjoying rain sound.
Awesome, inexhaustible being
flowing over contours of body
running in rivulets
down the drain of yesterday.

Ever present.
The whole creation singing
I AM.

Give yourself to Love,
only Love
still, peaceful, empty.
No qualification

I love the animal body of myself
The way it shits and reads at
the same time

The way it crawls under covers and
beds down breathing under sheets
I love the way bare arms are warmed
and sitting happens—and writing.
All these wonders of the animal body
and the Knowing that feeds it
and clothes it
putting socks on its feet and
deciding this one, or that one, or none.

This figment of consciousness that
hears the bird and the pen
scratching at the same time.
It remembers eating and shitting
and loves the whole
fucking thing

I Am

a diamond; a glint
of mica; a star
a thing of immense value

I am the Source interacting with
itself as finite mind
but here's the thing:
I Am The SOURCE ITSELF!
Not in appearance. Not in thought.
But that. THAT gives the energy,
the soup—the essential Being
GOD
Knowing Its works through this
self knowing—body-mind
World.

It became clear as day that I is
an illusion. Even those words
unspoken were heard.
Like a mirage it shimmered and
appeared real—only when it
was not present could the difference
be discerned

Without a hint of I—no subject,
no object— "I" creates duality.
Feeling the sensation of pressure
and vibration arises the face
and from there a short distance
to the legs and feet and world
I'm a body!

A beam of Light
Love expresses itself in birdsong
Signaling through air and hearing
I am here—you are here
we are both here
Here being what we are—
expressions of Divine Majesty
The nth power.

Miraculous
I take it in
like the boy who swallowed
the ocean

A shadow on the grass
illustrates my bull-shaped head
This is mental—
equivalenting this form from
a shadow.
Also, a chair shape.
This is happening!
The mountain shape rises and dips
and rises again—
yet stays still.
What is moving?

It's a challenge to slip out of the
good/bad, black/white, either/or
concept that we're conditioned to
believe and that frankly is easier
than the quantum mechanics
of particles interacting and wave
function in the everyday world.

We discover as we suspend belief and
venture further into awareness being
what is without labels, explanations,
and definitions, that there is nothing
to be believed. That in fact, belief
doesn't matter and only keeps us caged
in a tight, seemingly secure
but actually ignorant loop of life
that maintains limits that keep us afraid
of living and dying.
Or at least keeps us suffering.

Many, like myself, seek escape from this
stifling worldview only to fall into the trap
of an opposing dogma.

The impulse is divine
the snags and traps many.
We're trained to think in absolutes
dualisms—either/or, this or that
and what if we learn neither, none, or many

who are we then?
Who will I be?

And here's the cosmic joke:
You'll be who you've always been
The one who knows being before
and after the circumstances
and situations.

We will have to deal with
body/mind/world but now from a clear
plateau, a mountaintop that remains
unchanging and ever reliable—
the knowing of being before we
began to build the monument.
Same as ever: unchanged, unchanging,
untouched, and eternal.

♪ Who can ask for anything more ♪

The breezes' caress is so soft
yet bears the chill of winter's bite
I'm on the brink—stay out or go in.
Gentle sun warmth from behind
keeps me outdoors craving more
Flooded with joy and gratitude

Consciousness Is Itself Alive

Consciousness is alive!
This realization takes my breath away.

I mean the whole thing is consciousness
And we—body, tree, wind—are
appearances in it.
For they fill consciousness in the
moment but are made of consciousness
simultaneously
So there is only consciousness
Alive!

Writing about it tames it—It's not tame.
It's wildly alive. And yet, totally
peace—or peaceful.
Like love, it's all itself
Advaita—not two.

The Earth is deeply sourced.
There is enough for everyone
but greed doesn't know enough.
Thinking we're supposed to get something,
marking achievement.
That there is somewhere to get,
or something owed.
That we're set off on a race to some end,
that there are separate ones competing.
These misunderstandings and false
beliefs are deeply programmed
in the delusion.

Our nature is peace.
There's nowhere to get—except as curiosity
and intellect in exploration.
The Self we all are is borderless
Consciousness unlimited
How can we know this—but we know.
What we are beyond appearance
within appearance—without appearance.

The sun shines today—our star
She knows Herself as Light.

She is Being Herself—
be your self.
Be as you are.

Wholeheartedly received
the cure for loneliness.
Longing for connection the human
heart turns to God who
Herself is longing but doesn't know it,
knows only the longing and the
fulfillment together. One.

I would go to my mother's house
and be joyously received.
Even on the day of her death
her memory shortened to now
she'd fall asleep for cat naps
awaken, see me at her bedside,
greet me joyously–
"Shirkale" she'd smile,
As if it was the first time, every time.
Truly loved and seen.
Her final words that day:
"Give my love to who you love."

Knowing

Made an instrument of thy Peace
With the Love that thou art. I Am.
Every fiber lit by your Light
In the echoing chamber silence resounds.
Every breath a prayer

Healed

Take your stand as possibility
A way of seeing;
Neither deflation nor inflation
In the wild unexplored territory of Being

This mind is a tool of creation
Through this finite mind the
universe appears and expands
Oh, to be attuned to nature's web
and power is to be truly alive

Outside my door
a welcoming mat of snowy petals
Small round whiteness of
softness carpet the entrance,
blowing and gathering in the wind.

The very tall cleveland pear tree
fills the front yard and sheds its glory.
A squirrel climbs the dogwood.
Just being itself.

Be Yourself

Be as you are:
Unlimited Being.
Wild stable beauty
Yourself.

I can feel a waning of energy
harder to walk and breathe
Let me finish this book so I can fly home
to the land of no-experience, no object.

There is a great blooming of trees and
leaves—a gentle wind caresses the
new leaves. Blossoms shine white
and I must do some planting.

Love, beauty, intelligence. The
currents of Awareness
the honey of beeing human.
Today is the solar eclipse
the darkening of the light in midday
a moment of reverence and appreciation
for the light.
Given so generously—the outpouring of
radiance to our beleaguered spirits
signaling return—again and again.
Steady constant sun divinely orchestrated.
A band of light across
the cobalt sky draws my eye.

We are made of Light.
It is the means and the substance.
Still empty, radiant, transmission.
The longing of the heart for
happiness: vibrating, kaleidoscopic.

Mindbody is one with the whole,
reflected in the world,
mirroring the deep desire of your heart.
To know and follow the one
is self potentiated, self fulfilled:
impersonal, infinite, intimate.

Today we have a cosmic event
that encourages people to look up

and celebrate the return of the light.

Deep gratitude fills the heart at the return
and awe at the display.
This everyday occurrence of the light
is celebration.
The mysterious magical ongoing return
to You as the universe.

Ho Hum

It's just an ordinary day.
Billions of people are donning special glasses
and looking at the sky.
Traffic halts
cities on the meridian are overrun
with enthusiasts.
Another meeting of moon and sun—
union of planet and her star—
apparent to our gaping gaze.
Hurray! we shout, silent with reverence
And then, traffic resumes, we go home
and forget.

Responsiveness

In the stillness buzzing actively
silent, continuous transmission
Heart to heart, mind to mind
like the functioning of the body as a whole
the very universe is intimately connected.

Do you feel alone, outside the world?
It is a deeply felt illusion—
real, but only a passing appearance.
Now here, now gone—
shrug off the cage of culture and be free.

Nothing is separate—certainly not you.
The very air you breathe passes
through my lungs.
Imagine the intricate messages
from being to being circling the globe.
It is your voice magnified to the seven
billionth degree.

This is your home. You belong here.

Open all the pores of your face
to the kinship that surrounds us
We are all the same substance
made of light and love.
We just got stuck inside this cage
and can't see the door is wide open.

Step into the unknown.
You are strangely sturdy on two feet
Wave your arms around, there is room.
You flutter in air like a bird but
remain grounded.
Take a morsel of dirt in your mouth,
you're made of that. It tastes earthy.
Remember who you are. Your divine nature.
You are needed.

We're all mourning somebody
or something. Nothing lasts.
Time's illusion remembered
or imagined.
The candy bowl of three or four wrappers
a faint fragrance—conjured taste
of sticky sweetness.

Even the fullness of sex entering the body
It's the smoke of memory:
Mother, father, sister
the shower, the towel
the disagreements.
Vanished and relieved
vanquished.
The moaning of the wind gathers the ghosts—
soon, soon I'll join them

We are part of the dream of seasons.
You see how they turn and renew
Grow old, fall and rot.
Were they even there—
Where is there?

I'm an illusion too—
an aware illusion.
Right in keeping with creation,
passing through,
appreciating, loving the passage.

While I'm here I know I'm made up
by consciousness
Who is there to mind?
I'm the larger whole
seeing the scene
I'm the seeing. The Being
the One.
Just loving the whole thing.

I'm no different than the trees,
the green, the flowering, the sky,
the mountain
the world.
I am the Light.

I don't identify with being human
anymore
I identify with the whole
The One.
So when this seeing passes
you'll have my words.

The flowers have appeared on the
dogwood branches, sweet
sweet as ever.
The maple limb bows with red
clusters, soon to turn to leaves.
Wind sweeps through this greening season
Light shining, wind howling
blue sky, white clouds.
Incredibly beautiful

The maple bark is desiccating.
Naked smoothness beneath rough bark
I just want it to last as long as
I'm here; then it can rot.
I feel as one with that tree
Mother maple.
Forsythia gone to green.
The poplar stands straight.
There is a poplar above my grave site.
Long may it last!

You are the I Am of Yourself
Let no teacher say you don't exist.
Simply find out what this you is—
do this for yourself.
You are in good company—with
yourself.

This is not the "story" of you—
fascinating as you might find it.
Don't plumb into your memory
for yourself. You do not live there—
only the ghosts of Christmas past.
Where you are now, as you are now
cannot be anywhere else.
There is nowhere to look that you are not

What is this you that is always present
the very you of yourself.
One that knows—is aware
empty, clearly lucid, transparent, here.
That is yourself.

It is not a person.
It is not a body-mind though it
makes good use of them
It is before and after and now
It is yourself.

Nothing to do about it.
Nothing needs to be done about it.
This understanding turns everything
on its head—upside down
downside up—down upside
updownside—what!!!
I'm definitely here—but as what?!
Awareness in a body.
Holy smoke!

There is no separate I
There is awareness, consciousness,
the only I.
Appearing as a zillion things.
Including me, this.
Transcending this I am Self, One,
God Being,
Light.

Floating, being alive
Fabulous. In and out.
Always myself
Empty, open, present
boundless.

There is no I, no separate I
A chimera

Portal

We enter portals through each other
Discerning an expanse of Self
Passing from dance partners to the
dance itself
Interweaving
along the chain of Being.

The rough return to the body's heat
feels coarse
Fingers probing physical portals
are "down to earth."
In the dream the transaction is tender
the memory swoony—
the caress safe.

At the hairdresser we unexpectedly
speak of entering God
becoming One—knowing God.
On the massage table the
relaxation of body brings expanse.
The organ recital sounds strangely
like orgasm.

Where and how the portals open
and fall away is a surprise.
I am left weightless:
myself, just a memory.

The freedom. There is no one to appease.
No one to appeal to. Only myself.
Only the One.

The light filtering through leaves
seems to move.
Leaves sway and flutter:
leaf language.
Conversation with the wind.
You think it is only words that speak?
Blossoms lie scattered on the ground.
Mute. It is all speaking the
language of silence
Whatever moves me moves the world

Blossoms continue to fall
A huge winged creature appears, descends
disappears
How to describe "at once."
The world lightens.
"I am a movement and a rest"

AC-DC

I love my human nature
I do.
The Divine and human,
Impersonal and personal,
are connected in Love
This holy marriage sometimes falters
when we get too wrapped up
in one or the other.
The beauty, love and intelligence
bestowed upon the world
created by consciousness through we humans
gets all bolluxed up
with judgment, hate, and ugliness
but remains love, beauty and
intelligence at its core.
We have courage—that is the heart.
The alternating current and direct
current of our electric being.

"To the eyes of a man with imagination
  Nature is imagination itself"
                            -William Blake

"The way we see the world can restore
  its soul and the way the world is ensouled
  can restore our vision"
                            -Patrick Harpur

Similar to the idea of bringing divinity back into the world
through the recognition of the One.

Safe and Unbound

Poet, mystic from a long strain
of these molecules. Connecting
somewhere in the unbound
universe, irrespective of DNA
Beyond genomic ancestry,
daughter of the fairies where home
is Ireland, The Amazon, The Caucasus
We who fly.
Lights, sparkles of color, floating
orbs, scary faces, powerful
legions, sprinkle dust—beware!
Held in these bodies, with
arms and legs, not a bug, not
a deer, but a human form—
Simply form—hidden depths
of soul—not in and not outside the body
not in dimensionality
just Being, known.
A cell of the mother divine.

I feel the rightness of things,
experiences as they occur and to witness
and participate. Doesn't really say it
as it's realized—but it's the
way of the days unfolding.

The Isness beneath awareness
the silence beneath sound
supporting the cosmos.
The mind of God
I Am

The rain and wind supporting the tree
All appearance pointing to me, to me—
a movement
a breath
ingredient of Being
I see some blossoms
remain on the tulip poplar tree

Sound of the rain
a blanket of comfort
Sunk in sound:
connect, connect

Divine Harmony

Awareness touches the highest
blossoms on the poplar tree
and beyond
The blue tinted sky, the soft
white clouds
sails in the breeze.
A glorious day.
Who can make a day like this?
Only nature—she who made me
and you, and this we are.
The feeling below the beauty
or engendered by it—or Itself

The limbs hang so gracefully
Yellow orange blossoms perched
on sunlit green leaves
bowing and dancing to the sun

This seeing is grace itself
A butterfly—yellow and black
dashes by

The swishing music of leaves
caressed by wind
This I am. Being knowing Itself.
This I offer to the One.

Onesome

Remember yourself
before appearance
Ocean without waves
onesome

Because I am I get to participate
in this magical realm of Being
So interesting to natural intelligence
disguised this way by Nature

To live in the light means I get to
experience the light I am, that is
experienced when I close my eyes.
As pure Light and with open eyes
Marvelous world of appearance
Nature's bounty.

Beauty, Love, Intelligence: the
substratum of the Universe.

I like comparing myself to the
nematode— brethren. It keeps
me humble and also feels true—
and I'm glad, I'm me too.

Celebration

The mystery, the love, the power,
the beauty, the wholeness
As night approaches, daylight fades
the trees move in joyful abandon
to the music of rain and wind.
The dark leaves that have just come
into their maturity sway and
leap in their newfound glory
again.

See with the eye of God
manifest here on Earth
nothing hidden
nothing separate

Susurrus sound of Source
whispers through naked branches.
Pale green leaves newly formed
respond
So were we all born
clinging to arms
of the Mother

Body intimacy
deep body intimacy of awareness.
Overwhelmed by life
15 mo. old Rosa shrieks with fear
at the unexpected stranger in the living room
Clings to her mother, gives
this unwelcome stranger the stink eye.

Life big and life small

The whole vista of the universe beyond
world is imagined, the eye of awareness
Objectless– the subject a point
in the vastness, unlocated,
fearless

It all happens seemingly to a me.

a blue striped shadow
on the whitened earth.
palette for the day's wonder.

lit by morning sun
snow crystals sparkle
all colors of the rainbow

Stillness
a faint rumble in the ear
tiny tremble of a leaf
Nothing holds Its breath but
waits

I'm told the Earth is moving around the Sunstar
at incredible speed
That's funny

I'm not here for me. Not here for you.
Here for Her—the One who takes
many different forms. Shape shifts
in form and formless, arrives on a
chariot made of dreams and light—
announces herself in sleep and waking
and is only always One. I'll call her Durga because
that's how she whispered her name in my ear in
the moment between
waking and sleep.
I listened. I followed. I courted
and pursued and discovered her in
every grocery store and temple in Goa
and Mumbai, and I knew her in
Buddha's garden when he turned the
wheel of Dharma. And I am She.
I found her in my sunroom in Candler
and in my loins and feet and
toes that look like they're still baking
in primordial ooze.

This is the place of the Light—
our sun sees to this—and points beyond to our
sister stars and planets that graze the
Universe, as we call it, graze above
my head—which is a marvel in itself.

There is no way to describe the Truth.
It has to be known as Itself. Felt as
so itself that there is no wiggle room

to either side, neither above or below
Fills space and time—truth makes
Itself known without a doubt—with no
crack in the void for light—it is before
light—unmistakable reality—ab ovo
in the formless certainty of feeling
As experience. Embodied.
It is neither before or after—it is
complete surrender, destruction of ego,
Self unmistakable of the deepest Real.

This costume of me—its' psychology,
biology, spiritual beliefs, even its'
Philosophy is so cunning and grounded
So enjoyable and intense, its' suffering
and triumphs so pleasurable and
real seeming that it's addictive—
The attachments, the poetry, the Beauty
swoon-worthy.

"You can't have your cake and eat it too,"

Says Rupert. I rebelled but
it's true, probably. To give up
suffering in duality you do give up, it
seems, a certain human dimension for
the sake of truth. For Durga for
Myself.
The whole is not human.

October 7, 2023

"Dad, listen," the excited voice came through
on the audio. "I killed ten of them with my own hands
and I'm talking on the Jew's phone." "Do you hear Dad.
Ten of them, with my own hands,"
the translation continued.
His mother's tired voice: "Come home safe."

Raped, decapitated, burned: babies, pregnant women,
old, young, female, male, children, wheelchairs,
terrorized—the only requirement: Be a Jew.

On our campuses young Jewish female students
are afraid to leave their rooms. A jihad frenzy
has captivated the best and brightest
as if this massacre has moral equivalency
with Israelis defending their country.
Way beyond right and wrong or any dual concept.
Not political, not economic
No word for this ruthless, planned barbarism.
Like Vikings or goths sweeping down from
the coastal plains—A planned killing spree
fired by hatred and religious fanaticism.

I'm a Jew
All my Israeli cousins are Jews
All my dead relatives gassed and starved
and murdered in the nazi killing fields were Jews
My children are Jews

I'm an American Jew born and educated and grown
on Brooklyn soil. I believed I was safe.
That my children were safe.
That my relatives were safe.
As safe as we could be in this uncertain world
But now there is a certainty:

That the hatred and murderous actions against Jews can
be rationalized, explained away as if it is normal
Palestinians doing the planned killing instead of terrorists
who use their own children and women as shields.

Just scratch with your fingernail and find antisemitism
seething under the soil, this most ancient hatred, this
scapegoat used for centuries by power seekers to mine
peoples' ignorance and fear of death, lead them into
obedience by offering salvation with inflamed and
inflated visions of heaven and hell.

I've always been afraid of wearing a Star of David
around my neck. I've seen women and men
wear crosses with seeming abandon.
In elementary school I knew a teacher's hatred,
felt the spittle from her lips burn my skin
as she stood over my desk in a rage for no other reason
than I was a little Jewish girl that she was forced
to teach.

Flaming October
Pink and lavender sky
Purple mountain
Russet dogwood, red glory
Bright wind of evening
Awe

I Am inherently great.

What more is there than this
I am That.

The questioning that mind
likes to do is filler
kapok–fluff that flies away
in the light– hardly remembered
but in the moment of hearing seems
an answer. Trick of Mercutio.

All is the dream of the Divine.
Nature's love and power
is my conscious knowing,
nectar for the lips of God.
I can only hope so.
That this recognition awakens
impersonal divinity to Itself
To glory Itself.
To its wonderfulness.
And to my Love. One Love.

My mother said, her final
instruction, "Give my love to who you love."
And I do, mother. I do.

What a day! What a gift
The meadow whitened by snowfall
The frigid temperature of 28°.
Two days ago I sat in shirtsleeves
in the garden with the hot sun baking
my face—irresistible though risky—
and today, real winter.
So I can't go out, drive the car, buy food.
I have to stay in (oh fortunate pastime) and
wear a sweatshirt and read my book and Be
Secretly and totally delighted.
The dogwood now sits in a circle of white
Bare branches tipped with shining drops of ice.
Behind striped white and grey sky,
patches of blue,
luminous and shining.
Dripping leaves.
On a warm day soon I'll gather the scattered
fallen limbs the wind brought down.
Today, content with tea and book and pen
I just can't go anyplace.
The ground heaves, warm earth rising
secrets going on beneath the snow-patched grass.
The holly leaves shimmer and glisten
Everything is here.

The world opens and closes with me
I am given to myself in holy marriage

Wake up! Go to sleep.
It's all the same
dream
Standing, sitting, lying down.

What is the Nature of Consciousness or Being?

Impersonal, unbounded, Flowing,
intelligent, beneficent, Loving,
beautiful, magnificent, Patient,
Timeless, extravagant,
Infinitely creative; unashamedly Itself,
Spontaneous
totally Present—
omnipresent, Love Itself

And What Is The Nature Of The Body?

finite, limited, magnificent, self-healing,
functional, loving, sensitive, complex, creative,
changing, useful, serving, needy, beautiful, fleshy,
dumb, responsive, fun, alive, time-bound, built,
variable, subject to breakdown, intelligence—
strength, weakness

It's a wild situation—the world
is like the body

abide as the endless ocean
but what is prior
That is what I Am

Already and forever here.
Whether the form be out or seen
Being is.
It's a different headset knowing
what's happening is an appearance
of reality. That reality is ongoing and
unchanging. Enjoy the view.
Lighthearted, it's fun to be alive.

A conundrum
though not separate—I am
and so are you.
The body is, but I am not body
The tree is, but I am not the tree
The wind is, I'm not the wind.
I am aware being—though in form
I am not the form
Though the form appears in me—
What is this me and you if not separate?
And since not separate—since separate is
just a thought—
not reality.
Who thinks? Thinking thinks.
Perceiving perceives—there is not a one
only One
and you are that. So am I

There is a stream flowing
invisible to the eye, felt in awareness
The joining of heaven and earth
The I Am here now–movement and rest
Inexhaustible Being–Mind everywhere
Love, Beauty, Intelligence.

Don't segment yourself–brother to the worm–this
body is not immortal.
Leave that to the planaria.
We are evolving continually.
I'll go anywhere I'm called.
Already home between
Heaven and Earth.

Of With as The Light (of Being)

The link of heaven and earth
I stand—akin to the light of Being
and nature's tool.
As above so below
while Hermes scuttles between
ever the charming or malevolent trickster

Oh, Nature decides as she rushes
through these evolved cells
Molecules at her bidding
I learn to attend.
One of the Light, with the Light
As the Light.
The source of Nature's plaything

We stand erect—head to the stars,
feet on the ground.
The wisdom of this design.
In the end Nature has her way
but the soul ascends up and out,
into the Oneness it has always been

There is no time in Being
neither time nor space–
this is entirely Nature's domain.
But the knowing, the knowing that
I am the Light of aware Being–
Peace and happiness abide.

I gave myself away for tinsel
Before I knew true value.
Not knowing is a dangerous sport,
builds in itself and grows,
desperate to feel valued.
"Don't cast your pearls before swine,"
my analyst said.
But how to know who is worthy
when I didn't know myself
Sitting on a pot of gold
but blind.
It's taken time to learn
what is value—
Love based in being.

The trees and the wind speak to me
The space between the leaves make music
The birds sing in harmony
I sit in mute appreciation
full to the brim.
Everything is green. The color of wisdom.

We put words to experience
expressing this natural being
Days of peace, abundance
Nature is so effulgent
she bursts with generosity
The green, the hedges, the trees
are over the top.
Right in your face: beauty, beauty, beauty.
And this is all of us.
Arms laden, how much can I take—
unlimited nature.
Boundless presence
Bow down and kiss her feet.

La Vie En Rose

Last night lying in my bed I realized
that I love myself so much. I whisper
Te quiero and I'm speaking love words
to my Being, to the true self I am
that I love so much and the
words of La Vie En Rose, in English,
seem to express my feelings of and
toward this One Being that I Am

"And when you speak angels sing from above
 Everyday words
 seem to turn into
 love songs

 Give your heart and soul to me ♪
♪ and life will always be La Vie En Rose"

It looked like wings
Could only be wings to this evolved eye
But it was I. The only One perhaps.

What is this perhaps—and what am I—
and does this knowledge lie with me
I call it soon
but that is just a way of comforting myself.

How to live in this eternity now.
I must have Love. Be Love.
Have always been Love.
It is my nature. Beyond Body.

Beyoncé. Now I understand.
There are many of us.

I was told my purpose was to live
in the Light.
That, and the wings, made clear
What I am, the One.
And I have been longing for someone
To tell me, someone to tell.
I'm telling now with this vast
Understanding that I can't grasp.
But if you hear me, if you grok—
I'll get it too.

Out of the Divine Light
which I Am
Came Evolution
which I am
And here now between heaven and earth
I am
Reconciling this anomaly
which I am

Consciousness the handmaiden
guiding the way
From the finite to the infinite
(and even as I write I feel my claws,
 now toes—retaining their prehensile
 grip—the tender pinky at the outer edge)

But there is no limit to the boundless
being that I am—lives within
this body that is ever changing,
not the thing itself but its meaning,
The Source.
At the explosion of the Big Bang I was
and still am
in faint memory. I feel the vibration.

When Love was needed it arose,
emergent from the ribs of body
and Being silent in the room
Thundering.

I am blessed and so many with me are blessed.
Alive in this beautiful natural world. It's easy
to focus on the miserable, the poor, the aging,
the sickness—but I have been instructed
to live in the Light and it is my blessing to do so.

What can I do for the planet? Do
is the inappropriate word. How can I be
as the planet, for the planet, in the planet,
on the planet—What does Nature ask
this denizen of hers to realize,
to know, to carry lightly? I wait consciously
to be told by this extravagant voice
that only I can hear—It is for me alone
And not for me but for Her, She who
moves within me, what I recognize as
me through familiarity.
I have been blessed to know myself for 86 years.
And every right turn has been given
And every wrong turn has been mine.
And so much love and so much suffering
in the Photo album of memory. What a ride!
And guided all the time by that
dark void within where truth lives,
and who I am eternally.

How can I give back? This writing is an effort,
meagre in comparison to the enormous richness
of even this day—laden with sunlight and rain
birdsong and video games

fancy solitaire but fun.

I am basically alone, connected
and intimately part of every being on the planet,
possibly the whole universe—but still that sense
of me: meta conscious.

We've come this far. How much further
does nature want to go? What can I
carry forth after this skin is shed?
I want to give it all, and take it all.
Fully fulfilled, I'm doing my best.
But perhaps I should stop eating meat entirely.
Somehow that doesn't feel right. I eat fish.
And plants.
And grass-fed animal products like
eggs and butter and cheese. I don't want to
give that up.
I'm not called to do so.

Today the bird song sounded especially
Pungent and meaningful–aware
that these were once dinosaurs
that roamed the earth terrifying
all creatures. Today their song
resounds sweetly on the ear.

Integration

There is nothing
I wish to get away from
or to

There is a wholeness to being; you
turn the kaleidoscope an inch to
the right and the pieces of color
arrange themselves into a pattern
of wholeness. A particle and a wave.
This is continuously happening—all
at once. Not in time. Though we don't
comprehend this eternity in our timed lives.

I sing La Vie En Rose in my bed at night—
Adoration of The One. The melody and
words linger in the mind for days—a
reminder. Today I read a library book
that I borrowed by chance and there it is—
La Vie En Rose! Words in a paragraph.

As long as I kept my wildness I could
touch my being. Once I submitted to
family I was lost.

"Child of nature, let them rail."

The unexpected, the imaginative, the
surprise. The emergent.

"It's all arranged," but not in any order
that can be anticipated.
It's not our order but the order of wholeness.

O' fat lovely leaves of the poplar tree
We are alive!

Dreaming the One

brings Her into Being
and I am redeemed
through Love.
We are together
clasped into each other
One again.

Time enters the realm
in a single thought
Ties it together
from zero to naught
Enters the world
made real
made flesh
material.

Words are the symbol
hint at meaning
There is no meaning
except itself
Like the media's message
the symbol the meaning
The fact that it is
is the thing in itself

God is the One
I'm part of the whole
Whole in itself
and God in the part
Live in the Light
the voice through the mind
Dead or alive
I'm not hard to find

Right here and now
eternally True
as you find yourself
I find me in you
We never were two
that too was a dream
a bold trickster scheme

Don't seek to understand
You already know
I am you, you are me
there's nowhere to go
And God is so happy
in knowing the Self
Pass into consciousness
Dream of Yourself

There is integrity in the quantum field
that cannot be replicated—that is
working, happening, functioning on its
own—and that we are representing and
being simultaneously.
It filters to the space-time continuum,
where we—the biological—live and know
through knowing of self as entity
is neither time nor space.

Arlie's question—or quest—to be
entirely without a trace—a scintilla
of the me paradigm——is this possible?
Or just the noting of it whenever it arises
Who cares? If it's for some future gain—
like freedom from suffering physical pain,
then it's in vain.
If it's for any attainment which implies
future then it's suspect.
Peace is now.
This is discovery.

The personality formed in the process of living,
the psychology or character that appears,
field of meta–psychology, myth, archetype,
human consciousness, evolutionary programming,
appreciated as the dynamic sphere.
Individual differences and qualities
within a prism, patterns generated
in a kaleidoscope,
the one mind or Consciousness of God.
We are all Brahman.
To experience this totality is beyond
mind's understanding, beyond the conceptual.

Gate Gate Pāragate Pārasamgate
Bodhi Svāhā

Acknowledgments

My deepest gratitude to the universe, to truth, beauty, and love. My deep thanks to Erin Brown, without whom this book would never have come into manifestation. To my children, who have showered me with endless love, and to the teachers, guides, and friends along the way who have helped me keep my ass on the cushion so that I could discover myself, for myself.